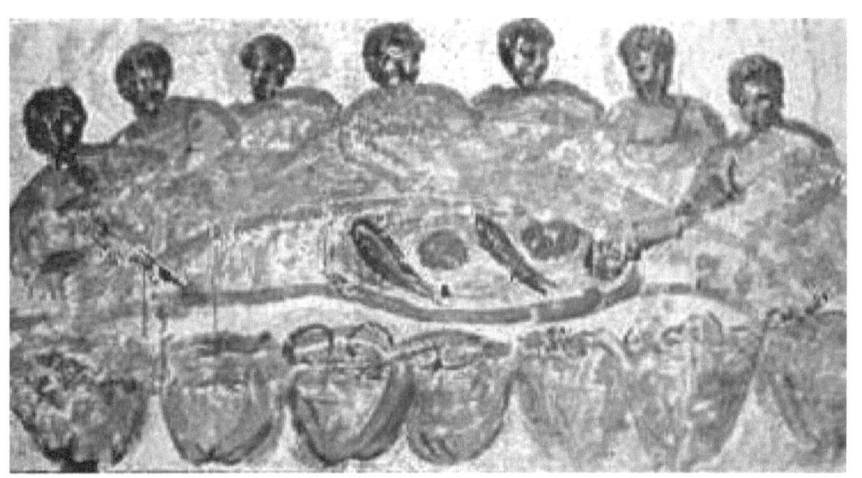

RITUAL
of HOPE

IDJC Press
idjc.org

For Where Two or Three Are Gathered in My Name There Am I in the Midst of Them.

Matthew 18:20

Ritual of Hope
Copyright © 2024
Stephen Joseph Wolf
All rights reserved.
No part of this book may be copied or reproduced in any form or by any means without the written permission of the publisher, except for the inclusion of brief quotations in a review or when needed for home prayer.

Stephen Joseph Wolf is retired, a former pastor and parish priest (22 lents & holy weeks), spiritual director and retreat leader, vocation director, dean, and college of consultors member, and former certified public accountant (14 tax seasons), and before that worked as a landscaper, desk clerk, laundry worker, janitor, paper boy, and student.
He sings baritone with the LGBTQ chorus Nashville in Harmony, plays the ukulele for Music for Seniors, is a volunteer bookkeeper for two non-profits, and is active in PFLAG Nashville, where he lives with his beloved husband Billy.

Cover art is a detail of an early Christian painting of an agape meal found in catacombs below Rome, from Wikimedia.

ISBN   978-1-937081-86-7   this paperback edition
       978-1-937081-87-4   hardcover edition

For more visit **www.idjc.org/ritual-of-hope/**

RITUAL of HOPE

Scripture	4
Introduction	5
AGAPE MEAL PRAYERS	8
EUCHARSTIC PRAYER	
Greeting & Penitential Rite	11
Gloria	12
Opening Prayer	13
Optional Scripture Readings	14
Nicene Creed	18
Prayers of the Faithful	19
Blessed are you…	19
APOSTOLIC TRADITION	20
Lord's Prayer	24
Sign of Peace	25
Fractioning & Communion	26
Prayer After Communion	27
ANAPHORA of ADDAI & MARI	28
Blessing of a Baby in the Womb	34
BAPTISM	35
CANDIDACY for CONFIRMATION	42
Blessing of a New Driver	48
MARRIAGE	50
Blessing of Married Couples	56
Prayers for the Sick	60
Blessing of Teachers & Students	62
Blessings of Advent Wreath	63
Blessing of Nativity Scene	63
Blessings of a Bible & a Vehicle	64
Blessings of a Mother & a Father	65
Commendation of the Dying	66
VIGIL for the DECEASED	68
FUNERAL at a GRAVESIDE	72
Prayers for Vocations	86
Blessing of Water	88
Universal Prayers of the Faithful	89

SCRIPTURE

If you do not have a home missal, mass readings are available at https://bible.usccb.org/daily-bible-reading.

These scripture passages are rendered for meditation from the three sources and other sources referenced in the eight books listed below.

Exodus 16:4-5,9,10b	*Bread from Heaven*	14
Psalm 23	*The Lord is my Shepherd*	75
Psalm 116:12-18	*The Blessing Cup*	15
Isaiah 25:6a,7-9	*The Veil that Veils*	74
Matthew 5:2-10	*The Beatitudes*	16
Matthew 24:3;25:34-36,37b,40	*Works of Mercy*	17
Mark 1:9-11	*Baptism of the Lord*	16
Luke 2:29-32	*Canticle of Simeon*	66
Luke 24:13-16,28-35	*Two of Jesus' Disciples*	76
John 14:1-6a	*In My Abba's House*	76
Romans 8:35,37-39	*What can separate us?*	51
1 Corinthians 11:23-25	*He Took Bread*	16
2 Corinthians 5:1,6-9	*Earthly Tent-House*	69

The Interlinear NIV Hebrew-English Old Testament, by John R. Kohlenberger III, Copyright © 1979, 1980, 1982, 1985, 1987 by the Zondervan Corporation

The NRSV-NIV Parallel New Testament in Greek and English, by Alfred Marshall, Copyright © 1990 by the Zondervan Corporation

The New Greek-English Interlinear New Testament, translators Robert K. Brown & Philip W. Comfort, Copyright © 1990 by Tyndale House Publishers

For other meditation renderings by Stephen Joseph Wolf see:

A Jesus Breviary, includes Jesus Incarnate, Sayings of Jesus, Miracles, Parables, the Paschal Mystery, the Holy Spirit, and Christian Living
31 Days of God's Love-Call, Old Testament passages on the love of God
Rainbow Psalms in 30 Days, with Canticles and Sayings of Jesus
Rainbow Prayer, with the commons of the saints and psalms of St. Francis
Dawn & Dusk Rainbow Prayer, in a two-week cycle for the full year
Dawn & Dusk Rainbow for Ordinary Time, in a two-week cycle
A Simple Family Breviary, arranged by month, season, and day of the week
Gone Before Us, praying for the dead
and eleven six-chapter books for faith-sharing

Visit **www.idjc.org**.

INTRODUCTION

This work has emerged from efforts to attend Mass then having to leave with a deep sadness that does not easily go away, and the awareness that I am not alone in this. This book is not intended for anyone who is able to happily participate in the sacramental life of the Church, nor is it intended to encourage anyone to stop doing so. As a faithful Catholic has a right to the sacraments, this ritual is for those faithful members of the People of God who are finding themselves unable to do so and still yearning to, a way to help those of us who feel pushed to the margins.

In other words, the purpose of this little book is to help faithful Catholics stay in the Church. Well-meaning friends invite me to join their denominations. Hard to say why, but I am still Catholic.

The core of this ritual is our identity as priests in the common priesthood of Jesus. Each baptized follower of Jesus the Christ has been anointed **priest, prophet**, and **royal**. As vassal **kings and queens** of the King of kings and queens, each of us has been gifted with power rooted in the *imago dei*, being created in the image of God with gifts and talents we are meant to use to wash the feet of humanity and participate in God's ongoing creative and healing work. As a **prophet** each of us will be called to speak a truth that God wants heard by a person, a community, or by the whole world, and speaking this truth will involve risk. As a **priest** in the common priesthood of Jesus the Christ, each of us is called to be in a personal relationship with the one God and to be in communion with God along with each human we encounter. And as priests we are given the power and duty to forgive, a power we use in the first place at home.

The *Agape Meal Prayers*, probably from the late 1st century AD might be best suited today for what we call a potluck supper or dinner on the ground, where everyone brings what they have and there is equal sharing, or perhaps for large family reunions. *Agape* is one of the Greek words for love. Scholars suggest that the words of institution were omitted to distinguish it from the Sunday Eucharist.

The *Eucharistic Prayer* is from the *Apostolic Tradition*, from about 215 AD, the prayer that I use regularly in these days.

The *Anaphora of Addai & Mari*, probably also from the 3rd century, is still the core of some Eastern Eucharistic Prayers. Like the *Agape Meal Prayers*, it did not originally have the words of institution, though they were later added by some traditions.

OPTIONS for STUDY and EXPERIMENTATION

We hear stories of priests who have been persecuted and faithful Christians in exile offering simple prayers over whatever food and drink is available. And yet everything eucharistic is meant to happen in a community; this is of course the ideal. And so anyone who uses the **Apostolic Tradition** and/or the **Anaphora of Addai & Mari** is encouraged to be aware of all the many ways each human being exists as a person-in-community, including with family and friends, and to continue to seek ways of being an apostle in the world.

Catholic rituals have many options, often with instructions to use *these or similar words*. Options are given here as incomplete introductions for consideration and study.

While a deacon, priest or bishop is the ordinary minister of **Baptism**, in cases of necessity even a non-Christian with the intention of doing so for the Church can baptize as long as water and the words (*I baptize you in the name of the Father and of the Son and of the Holy Spirit*) are used. Anyone who does so is advised to inform the local parish that this has happened with the correct words.

For all of the prayers, see *Order of Baptism of Children (Participation Booklet)*, ICEL, 4+X6+ inches, 80 pages, $4.95, Catholic Book Publishing Corp.

As a pastor I developed a **Candidacy for Confirmation**, used sometimes at a Sunday Mass and sometimes at the end of a Confirmation retreat, and offer it here as a way for a sponsor and parents to help a young person prepare for the sacrament. Some of it came from an article in one of the Catholic magazines.

The ritual for **Marriage** can be used by an officiant of a civil marriage. It recognizes that the officiant, whether priest or mayor, is the chief witness to the marriage while the spouses themselves confer the sacrament of marriage onto each other in their mutual exchange of consents, and it is their identity as priests in the common priesthood of believers that empowers them to do so. Most of this is what my husband and I used.

For all of the prayers, see *The Order of Celebrating Matrimony*, ICEL, 7+X10+ inches, 164 pages, $27.95, Catholic Book Publishing Corp.

With apologies, I have lost track of my source for the accompanying *Blessing of Married Couples*. I used it on Sundays preceding lovebird day, February 14.

The *Prayers for the Sick* and the *Commendation of the Dying* are not to take the place of the Sacrament of Anointing, but recognize that there will be times when a priest is not available.

For all of the prayers, see the book which is especially helpful for any layperson in parish ministry: ***A Ritual for Laypersons***: *Rites for Holy Communion and the Pastoral Care of the Sick and Dying*, 4+X6+ inches, 176 pages, $29.95, Liturgical Press.

For the other *Blessings* in this book, as with any blessing by the lay faithful, the leader simply signs theirself with the sign of the cross along with everyone else.

For more blessing prayers for the lay faithful, see *Catholic Household Blessings and Prayers*, USCCB, 6 X 9 inches, 528 pages, $26.95, Catholic Book Publishing Corp.

Though a *Funeral* is normally presided over by a priest or deacon, a graveside funeral can be done by anyone. Sometimes a family would prefer that one of their members lead the prayers of Committal on the four pages beginning on page 82. It was disheartening to hear during the pandemic that some people had a hard time getting a priest to do a graveside service.

For all of the prayers, see *The Funeral Rites (Participation Booklet)*, ICEL, 4+X6+ inches, 80 pages, $5.50, Catholic Book Publishing Corp.

If prayer is done with a group of people, consider making copies and inviting all present to read the prayers together.

From the institutional church I beg patience and forbearance with all of this. I know this is not easy. Please remember that Catholics who feel marginalized are also being asked to continue being patient with our institutional church.

Stephen Joseph Wolf
January 3, 2024

AGAPE MEAL PRAYERS

(from the *Didache*, late 1st century)

THANKSGIVING BEFORE AN AGAPE MEAL

WINE POURED

We give you thanks, Abba,
for the holy Vine of your servant David,
whom you have made known to us
through your Son Jesus;
to you is the glory forever.   R. **Amen.**

BREAD BROKEN

We give you thanks, Abba,
for the life and knowledge
which you have made known to us
through your Son Jesus;
to you is the glory forever.   R. **Amen.**

As this broken bread
scattered on the mountains and
being gathered together became one,
so may your People be gathered together
from the ends of the earth into your reign,
for yours is the glory and the power
through Jesus Christ forever.   R. **Amen.**

ALL SHARE THE BREAD & WINE
AND THEN THE REST OF THE MEAL IS SHARED

THANKSGIVING AFTER THE MEAL
WHEN ALL ARE SATISFIED

We give you thanks, Holy Abba,
for your Holy Name, which you have caused
to dwell in our hearts, and for knowledge
and faith and eternal life, which you have
made known to us through your Son Jesus;
to you is the glory for ever.

You, Almighty Ruler,
created all things for your Name's sake,
gave food and drink for humans to enjoy
that we may give you thanks,
and you freely give us spiritual food and
drink and eternal life through your Son.
Before all things of creation
we give thanks that you are almighty;
to you is the glory for ever.

Remember, Lord, your Church:
deliver it from all evil, perfect it in love,
and gather it from the four winds into
your reign which you have prepared for it.
The cosmos may pass away;
let your grace come.

Hosanna to you, God of David;
to you is the glory and power through
Jesus Christ forever. Maranatha.   R. Amen.

EUCHARISTIC PRAYER

GREETING & PENITENTIAL RITE

\+ **In the name of the Father
and of the Son
and of the Holy Spirit.**

>R. **Amen.**

**May the peace of Christ,
the love of Abba,
and their communion in the Holy Spirit
be with us all.**

>R. **And with our Spirit.**

Aware of the love of God,
we call to mind our sins.

>(pause)

Lord, have mercy.	R. **Lord, have mercy.**
Christ, have mercy.	R. **Christ, have mercy.**
Lord, have mercy.	R. **Lord, have mercy.**

**May almighty God
have mercy on us,
forgive us our sins
and bring us to everlasting life.**

>R. **Amen.**

GLORIA
Sundays, Solemnities & Feasts (except Advent & Lent)

Glory to God in the highest,
and on earth peace and goodwill
to all people.
>We praise you, we bless you,
>we adore you, we glorify you,
>we give you thanks for your great glory,
>Lord God, Ruler of heaven and earth,
>O God, almighty Abba.

Lord Jesus Christ, Only Begotten Son,
Lord God, Lamb of God, Son of Abba,
>you take away the sin of the world,
>>have mercy on us;
>
>you take away the sin of the world,
>>receive our prayer;
>
>you are seated at the right hand of Abba,
>>have mercy on us.

For you alone are the Holy One,
>you alone are the Lord,
>you alone are the Most High, Jesus Christ,
>with the Holy Spirit,
>in the glory of God our Abba.

Amen.

OPENING PRAYER

ADVENT, CHRISTMAS, & EASTER

**Pour forth, we ask you, O Lord,
your grace into our hearts, that we, to whom
the Incarnation of Christ your Son was
made known by the message of an Angel,
may by his Passion and Cross
be brought to the glory of his Resurrection,
who lives and reigns with you in the unity
of the Holy Spirit, God for ever and ever.**

R. **Amen.**

LENT

**By your help, we ask, Lord our God,
may we be eager in that same charity
with which, out of love for the cosmos,
your Son handed himself over to death,**
   Through…　　　　　　　　R. **Amen.**

ORDINARY TIME

**Almighty ever-living God,
who govern all things in every place,
in your mercy hear your people calling
and bring your peace to our times,**
   Through **our Lord Jesus Christ, your Son,
   who lives and reigns with you
   in the unity of the Holy Spirit,
   God for ever and ever.**　　　R. **Amen.**

READINGS FOR THE DAY,
OR OTHER READINGS,
OR:

A HEBREW SCRIPTURE READING

A reading from the book of Exodus: 16:4-5,9,10b

The Lord said to Moses, "See, as I rain down for you bread from heaven, and the people will go out and gather enough each day for the day… But on the sixth day they will prepare what they bring in, to be twice what they gather day to day… Tell them I have heard the grumblings of the sons and daughters of Israel, and at evening you will eat meat and in the morning you will be filled with bread; then you will know I am the Lord your God."

In the evening quail came and covered the camp, and in the morning there was a layer of dew around the camp; when the dew went away, they saw on the desert floor thin flaking, thin like frost on the ground. When they saw it, they said to each other, "What is this?" (*man hu*?) They did not know.

So Moses said to them, "This is the bread that the Lord has given to you for food."

The word of the Lord.   R. **Thanks be to God.**

A RESPONSORIAL
as in Holy Thursday

PSALM 116:12-18

R. **Our blessing cup is a communion
with the blood of Christ.**
1 Corinthians 10:16

How can I repay to the LORD
for all the goodness done to me?
I will lift the cup of salvation
and call on the name of the LORD.

R. **Our blessing cup is a communion
with the blood of Christ.**

Precious in the eyes of the LORD
are the saints to the death.
I am your servant, the child of your servant;
you have freed me from the chains.

R. **Our blessing cup is a communion
with the blood of Christ.**

I will offer the sacrifice of thanksgiving
and call on the name of the LORD.
My vows to the LORD I will now fulfill
in the presence of all the people.

R. **Our blessing cup is a communion
with the blood of Christ.**

AN EPISTLE READING

A reading from the first letter of Paul
to the Corinthians: 11:23-25

I handed on to you what I received, that on the night the Lord Jesus was betrayed, he took bread and gave thanks and broke it saying, "This is my body for you; do this in remembrance of me."

In the same way the cup, after supper saying, "This cup is the new covenant in my blood; do this, as often as you drink, in remembrance of me."

The word of the Lord.   R. **Thanks be to God.**

A GOSPEL READING

A reading from the gospel of Mark: 1:9-11

In those days Jesus came from Nazareth of Galilee and was baptized in the Jordan by John. Right away going up out of the water he saw the heavens being opened and the Spirit as a dove coming down to him, and a voice out of the heavens: "You are my beloved Son, with you I am well pleased."

OR

A reading from the gospel of Mathew: 5:2-10

Jesus began to teach the crowds, saying
 "Blessed are the poor in spirit
    for theirs is the reign of heaven.

Blessed are those mourning
   for they will be comforted.
Blessed are the meek for they will inherit the earth.
Blessed are those hungering and thirsting
   for what is right; they will be satisfied.
Blessed are the merciful for they will obtain mercy.
Blessed are the clean of heart for they will see God.
Blessed are the peacemakers for they will be called
   sons and daughters of God.
Blessed are those persecuted for what is right,
   for theirs is the reign of heaven.

OR

A reading from the gospel
of Mathew: 24:3; 25:34-36,37b,40

Jesus said to the disciples in private, "The Ruler will say to the sheep, 'Come, you blessed by my Abba; inherit the realm prepared for you from the foundation of the cosmos. For I was hungry and you gave me to eat, I was thirsty and you gave me drink, I was a stranger and you welcomed me, naked and you clothed me, I was ill and you cared for me, I was in prison and you came to me." The just will say, "When did we?" And the Ruler will answer them, "Amen I tell you, what you did to one of the least of my brothers or sisters, you did to me.' "

The gospel of the Lord.
   R. **Praise to you, Lord Jesus Christ.**

NICENE CREED – Sundays & Solemnities

I believe in one God the Abba almighty,
> maker of heaven and earth,
> of all things visible and invisible.

I believe in one Lord Jesus Christ,
> the Only Begotten Son of God,
> born of the Abba before all ages.
> God from God, Light from Light,
> true God from true God, begotten, not made,
> one in being with the Abba;
> through him all things were made.
> For us and for our salvation he came from heaven,
> and by the Holy Spirit was

(bow) **incarnate of the Virgin Mary, and became human.**
> For our sake he was crucified under Pontius Pilate,
> he suffered death and was buried,
> and rose again on the third day
> in accordance with the Scriptures.
> He ascended into heaven
> and is seated at the right hand of the Abba.
> He will come again in glory to judge the living
> and the dead and his reign will have no end.

I believe in the Holy Spirit,
> the Lord, the giver of life, who proceeds
> from the Abba and the Son, who with
> the Abba and the Son is adored and glorified,
> who has spoken through the prophets.

I believe in one, holy, catholic and apostolic Church.
I confess one Baptism for the forgiveness of sins
and I look forward to the resurrection of the dead
and the life of the world to come. Amen.

PRAYERS of the FAITHFUL

**For ourselves and for all children of God,
we pray to the Lord...** R. Lord, hear our prayer.

For the needs of the Church, we pray...

For public authorities and the world, we pray...

For those oppressed by any need, we pray...

For our local community, we pray...

**All this we ask
through Christ our Lord.** R. **Amen.**

BREAD & WINE

**Blessed are you, Lord God of all creation,
for through your goodness
we have received this bread and wine:
fruit of the earth
and work of human hands,
to do what Jesus asked us to do.**

**Accept, Lord, the sacrifice we offer
from the blessings of creation
and the joys and sorrows of our lives,
for our good,
and for the good of all your people.**

CONTINUE WITH The APOSTOLIC TRADITION, on the next page
OR WITH The ANAPHORA of ADDAI & MARI on page 28.

APOSTOLIC TRADITION

(Eucharistic Prayer from 215 AD)

The Lord be with us.
> R. **And with our spirit.**

We lift up our hearts.
> R. **We lift them up to the Lord.**

We give thanks to the Lord our God.
> R. **It is right and just.**

We give you thanks, O God,
through your beloved Child Jesus Christ,
whom you sent as Savior, Redeemer,
and Messenger of your will,
your inseparable Word
through whom you created everything
and in whom you take great delight,
born of the Spirit and the virgin.

Doing your will,
to gain for you a holy people,
he stretched out his hands in suffering
to liberate from suffering
those who believe in you.

On the night he was to surrender himself
into voluntary suffering:
to dissolve death,
and break the chains of slavery,
and pour out his light,
and establish the covenant,
and manifest his resurrection,

he took bread,
blessed it with thanksgiving,
broke it,
and gave it to his disciples,
saying:

> TAKE AND EAT;
> THIS IS MY BODY,
> WHICH IS GIVEN FOR YOU;
> DO THIS IN MEMORY OF ME.

In the same way he took the cup,
blessed it with thanksgiving,
and gave it to his disciples,
saying:

> TAKE AND DRINK,
> ALL OF YOU,
> FOR THIS IS MY BLOOD
> OF THE NEW COVENANT,
> WHICH WILL BE SHED FOR YOU
> AND FOR THE MANY
> FOR THE FORGIVENESS OF SINS.
>
> DO THIS IN MEMORY OF ME.

As they sang a hymn of praise,
we too may sing:

> Holy, Holy, Holy Lord God of hosts.
> Heaven and earth are full of your glory.
> Hosanna in the highest.
> Blessed is he who comes
> in the name of the Lord.
> Hosanna in the highest.

Remembering
his Death and Resurrection,
we offer you the bread of life
and the wine of salvation,
and thank you for making us worthy
to be in your presence and serve you.

Send your Holy Spirit, we pray,
on the offering of your holy people,
to gather into one all who receive it.
May we be filled with the Holy Spirit
who strengthens our faith in the truth.
And may we be able to praise and glorify
you through your Child Jesus Christ.

> Remember all who have gone before us
> marked with the sign of faith;
> united with Jesus in a death like his,
> may they also be one with him
> in his Resurrection.

Through him, with him, and in him,
glory and honor to you,
Abba and Son, one with the Holy Spirit,
now and for ever! R. **Amen.**

THE LORD'S PRAYER

Taught by our Lord Jesus Christ
and being formed in his living word,
we pray:

**OUR FATHER, who art in heaven;
hallowed be thy name.
Thy kingdom come; thy will be done
on earth as it is in heaven.
Give us this day our daily bread
and forgive us our trespasses as we
forgive those who trespass against us,
and lead us not into temptation
but deliver us from evil.**

or Our Abba in heaven,
your name be honored
and your reign come
on earth as in heaven.
Give us bread for the day,
forgive us our sins as we forgive others,
and help us resist
temptation to do the bad
with grace to do the good.

Deliver us, Lord, we pray, from every evil,
graciously grant peace in our days.
In your mercy, keep us free from sin
and safe from distress and anxiety,
as we await the blessed hope and
the coming of our Savior, Jesus Christ.

R. **For the kingdom, the power, and
the glory are yours, now and forever.**

SIGN of PEACE

Lord, Jesus Christ,
who said to your Apostles:
Peace I leave you, my peace I give you,
graciously grant peace and unity
in accordance with your will,
who live and reign for ever and ever.
R. **Amen.**

The peace of the Lord be with us always.
R. **And with our spirit.**

Let us offer each other the sign of peace.

FRACTIONING

Lamb of God,
you take away the sins of the world,
have mercy on us.
Lamb of God,
you take away the sins of the world,
have mercy on us.
Lamb of God,
you take away the sins of the world,
grant us peace.

HOLDING the BREAD & WINE

As John the Baptist said at the river:
Behold the Lamb of God
who takes away the sins of the world.
Blessed are all who are called
to the supper of the Lamb.

COMMUNION

PRAYER AFTER COMMUNION

THE SEASONS

**Pour out on us, Lord, your Spirit of love,
and in your kindness
make those you have nourished
by the paschal meal
one in mind and heart
through Christ our Lord.**   R. **Amen.**

ORDINARY TIME

**Humbly we ask, almighty God,
be graciously pleased to grant
that those you renew with your Presence
may also serve with lives pleasing to you
through Christ our Lord.**   R. **Amen.**

FINAL BLESSING

The Lord be with us.

                      R. **And with our spirit.**

May almighty God bless us,
+ the Abba, and the Son,
   and the Holy Spirit.   R. **Amen.**

We go in peace.   R. **Thanks be to God.**

ANAPHORA of ADDAI & MARI
(Eucharistic Prayer probably from 3rd century
Edessa, Urfa in modern Turkey)

The Lord be with us.
> R. **And with our spirit.**

We lift up our hearts.
> R. **We lift them up to the Lord.**

We give thanks to the Lord our God.
> R. **It is right and just.**

PREFACE

**Worthy of praise from every mouth
and of confession from every tongue
is the adorable and glorious name
of the Abba and Son and Holy Spirit,
who created the world by grace
and its inhabitants by mercy,
saved by compassion
giving great grace to human beings.**

PRE-SANCTUS

To your majesty, O Lord,
a thousand thousands of those on high
bow down and worship,
and ten thousand times ten thousand
holy angels and hosts of spiritual beings,
ministers of fire and spirit,
praise your name
with holy cherubim and seraphim
shouting and praising without ceasing
and crying one to another and saying:

SANCTUS

Holy holy holy
Lord God of hosts.
Heaven and earth
are full of your praises.

POST-SANCTUS

With these heavenly hosts
we give thanks to you, Christ our Lord,
even we your humble servants,
for you have given us
great grace beyond recompense
in that you took on our humanity
to enliven it by your divinity,
and have exalted our humble estate
and restored our fall
and raised our mortality
and forgiven our trespasses
and justified our sinfulness
and enlightened our knowledge
and have condemned enmity
and, our Lord and our God,
granted victory
to our humble human nature
in the overflowing mercies of your grace.

OBLATION

O Lord, in your uncountable mercies,
for all our good and just ancestors
who have been pleasing in your sight,
make an acceptable memorial
in the commemoration
of the body and blood of your Christ
which we offer as you have taught us,
and grant us your tranquility and peace
all the days of the world.

May all inhabitants of the earth
come to know you,
that you are the only true God the Abba
and that you have sent
our Lord Jesus Christ your beloved Son.
He came and taught
in his lifegiving gospel
the purity and holiness of the prophets
and the apostles, martyrs, confessors,
bishops, doctors, presbyters, deacons,
and all the daughters and sons
of the holy catholic Church,
who have been signed
with the living sign of holy baptism.

ANAMNESIS

We also, Lord, your humble servants
who have received your example
which has been delivered to us,
are gathered in your name and presence
and now rejoice and praise and exalt
and commemorate and celebrate
this great and awesome and holy
and lifegiving and divine mystery
of the passion and death and burial
and resurrection of our Lord
and Savior Jesus Christ.

EPICLESIS

May your Holy Spirit come, O Lord,
rest upon this offering of your servants
and bless it and make it holy
that it may be to us, O Lord,
for the pardon of offences
and the forgiveness of sins
and for the great hope
of resurrection from the dead
and new life in the reign of heaven
with all those who have been
pleasing in your sight.

DOXOLOGY

For all this great and marvelous
dispensation toward us
we give you thanks
and praise without ceasing
in your Church redeemed
by the precious blood of your Christ,
with unclosed mouths and open faces
lifting up praise and honor
and confession and worship
to your living and holy
and lifegiving name
now and for ever,
world without end.   R. Amen.

CONTINUE WITH The LORD'S PRAYER on page 24.

BLESSING of a BABY in the WOMB

God, author of all life, bless, we pray, this child in the womb; give constant protection and grant a healthy birth as a sign of our rebirth one day in the eternal joy of heaven.

Lord, who have brought to this woman the wondrous joy of motherhood, grant her comfort in all anxiety and determination to lead her child along the ways of salvation.

[*For the father:*
Lord of the ages, who have singled out this man to know the grace and pride of fatherhood, grant him courage in this (*new*) responsibility, and make him for this child an example of justice and truth.]

[*For the family:*
Lord, you have put into the hearts of all people of good will a great awe and wonder at the gift of new life; fill this family with fidelity to the teachings of the Gospel and new resolve to share in the spiritual formation of this child in Christ our Savior, who lives and reigns for ever and ever.]

R. **Amen.**

BAPTISM

**Parents, in seeking to
have your child baptized,
you acknowledge
your responsibility of training them
in the practice of the faith
and how to love God and neighbor.
Are you ready for this?**

R. We are.

**Godparents, are you ready to help
in their ministry as Christian parents?**

R. We are.

**Family and friends,
you are invited to show by applause
your willingness to support this family.**

**Child, the Christian community
welcomes you with great joy.
In its name we claim you for Christ
our Savior by the sign of the cross
as your parents and godparents
now trace a cross on your foreheads.**

SCRIPTURE PASSAGE, PERHAPS MARK 1:9-11 on Page 16

INTERCESSIONS at BAPTISM

Brothers and sisters, let us ask our Lord Jesus Christ to look lovingly on this child about to be baptized, on *their* parents and godparents, and on all the baptized.

1. By the mystery of your death and resurrection, bathe this child in light, give *them* the new life of baptism, and welcome *them* into your holy Church. We pray to the Lord…

2. Through the sacraments, make *them* your faithful follower and a witness to your gospel. We pray to the Lord…

3. Lead *them* by a holy life to the joys of the reign of God. We pray to the Lord…

4. Make the lives of *their* parents and godparents examples of faith to inspire *them*, and keep *their* family always in your love. We pray to the Lord…

5. Renew the grace of our baptism in each one of us. We pray to the Lord…

LITANY of SAINTS

Holy Mary, Mother of God… R. Pray for us.
Michael, Gabriel and Raphael… "
All you Angels of God… "
Abraham, Moses and Elijah… "
All you Prophets of God… "
St. John the Baptist & St Joseph… "
St. Peter and St. Paul… "
Apostles, Disciples and Martyrs… "
_____ … "
All holy men and women… "
Christ hear us. Lord Jesus, hear our prayer.

PRAYER of EXORCISM

Almighty and ever living God,
   you sent your Son into the world to
   cast out evil, to rescue us from darkness,
   and bring us into the splendor
   of your reign of light.
We pray for this child:
   set *them* free from all sin,
   make *them* a temple of your glory,
   and send your Holy Spirit
   to dwell within *them*,
   through Christ our Lord. R. Amen.

Parents and godparents, by water and
the Holy Spirit this child is to receive
the gift of new life from God, who is love.
You will be *their* first teachers in
Christian living, *their* first catechists.
If your faith makes you ready for this,
renew now the vows
of your own baptism.
Reject sin;
profess your faith in Christ Jesus.
This is the faith of the Church,
the people of God, the Body of Christ.
This is the faith in which this child
is about to be baptized.

> Directing these questions
> to the parents and godparents,
> I invite everyone to respond "I do."

Do you renounce Satan?	R. I do.
And all his works?	R. I do.
And all his empty show?	R. I do.

Do you believe in God,
   the Abba almighty,
   Creator of heaven and earth? R. I do.

Do you believe in Jesus Christ,
   his only Son, our Lord,
   who was born of the Virgin Mary,
   suffered death and was buried,
   rose again from the dead
   and is seated at the right hand
      of the Abba? R. I do.

Do you believe in the Holy Spirit,
   the holy Catholic Church,
   the communion of saints,
   the forgiveness of sins,
   the resurrection of the body,
   and life everlasting? R. I do.

Parents, is it your will that your child
   be baptized in the faith of the Church?
                                          R. It is.

WITH WATER

N._____, I baptize you
in the name of the Father
and of the Son and of the Holy Spirit.

ANOINTING

**Child,
God the Abba of our Lord Jesus Christ
has freed you from sin, given you a
   new birth by water and the Holy Spirit,
and welcomed you into the holy people.
As Jesus the Christ was anointed
   Priest, Prophet and Ruler,
so may you live always as a member
   of his body sharing everlasting life.**

R. Amen.

Anoint Head in Silence.

CLOTHING with WHITE GARMENT

**Child,
   you have become a new creation,
   and have clothed yourself in Christ.
See in your white garment the outward
   sign of your Christian dignity.
With all those who love you
   helping you by word and example,
   bring that dignity unstained
   into the everlasting life of heaven.**

R. Amen.

BAPTISMAL CANDLE

Receive the light of Christ.

Parents and godparents,
> this light is entrusted to you
> to be kept burning brightly.

This child of yours
> has been enlightened by Christ.

They are to walk always
> as a child of the light.

May *they* keep the flame of faith
> alive in *their* heart.

When the Lord comes,
> may *they* go out to meet him with
> all the saints in the reign of heaven.

EARS & MOUTH

The Lord Jesus
made the deaf hear and the dumb speak.
May he soon
touch your ears to hear his word
and your mouth to proclaim his faith
to the praise and glory of God the Abba.
> R. Amen.

Let us welcome our newest member.

CANDIDACY for CONFIRMATION
Candidate, Parents & Sponsor

LED by the SPONSOR

**N., you came to the waters of baptism
because someone brought you to them.**

**You did not earn your creation;
your very being has been given to you
freely by our God and your parents.**

**You did not earn your baptism; your
baptism has been given to you freely
in the Body of Christ, the People of God.**

**I invite your parents, your first catechists,
to trace a cross on your forehead
as a reminder that you have been
claimed for Christ our Savior.** ☩

Parents trace a cross on the candidate's forehead with their thumb.

**I invite you as well to trace a cross
on your parents' foreheads,
as a sign of your gratitude.** ☩

I ask you now to lead your family and
  friends in renewing our baptismal
  promises by responding "I do."

APOSTLES CREED

Do you believe in God,
  the Abba almighty,
  Creator of heaven and earth?   R. I do.

Do you believe in Jesus Christ,
  his only Son, our Lord,
  who was born of the Virgin Mary,
  suffered death and was buried,
  rose again from the dead and
  is seated at the right hand
    of the Abba?   R. I do.

Do you believe in the Holy Spirit,
  the holy catholic Church,
  the communion of saints,
  the forgiveness of sins,
  the resurrection of the body,
  and life everlasting?   R. I do.

SPONSOR

N., Jesus gave us his body on the cross.
  You have gathered
  around the table of the Lord many times
  to do what Jesus asked us to do,
  eating and drinking the sacrament of life
  and saying your own Amen "Yes"
  to being a member of his Body.

I invite you to state your desire
  to keep growing as a disciple of Jesus,
  by responding *"I will."*

Will you prepare with mind and heart
and soul and strength to be sealed
with the gift of the Holy Spirit in
the sacrament of Confirmation?   R. I will.

Will you offer your best effort to respond
to God's love for you by seeking
to do good and avoid evil?   R. I will.

Will you trust in God's mercy
and confess your sins?   R. I will.

Will you give generous service to the
human family in imitation of Jesus, who
washed the feet of his disciples?   R. I will.

Will you be faithful in hearing and
following the teachings of the apostles,
in the breaking of the bread, and in the
prayer of the People of God?   R. I will.

Family and friends,
members of the Body of Christ,
please stand
as our candidate leads us in prayer.

**Loving Abba, help your universal
Church to be a leaven in the world and
to be the holy people you call your own;
We pray to the Lord…** R. Lord, hear our prayer.

**Help your faithful
who suffer persecution to
carry their cross in the footsteps of Jesus
and rejoice to be called Christians;
We pray to the Lord…** R. Lord, hear our prayer.

**Help us to work without ceasing
for the justice that brings
true and lasting peace;
We pray to the Lord…** R. Lord, hear our prayer.

**Stay close to our brothers and sisters who
are sick; Restore them to good health
and turn our worries for them into joy;
We pray to the Lord…** R. Lord, hear our prayer.

**Welcome all who have gone before us
into the reign of heaven
that they may see you face to face;
We pray to the Lord…** R. Lord, hear our prayer.

SPONSOR

N., I invite you to ask the Holy Spirit to take hold of your life with words you will hear in the sacrament of Confirmation:

CANDIDATE & SPONSOR

Almighty God,
  Abba of our Lord Jesus Christ,
  you brought me your servant to
  new birth by water and the Holy Spirit,
  freeing me from sin:
Send upon me, O Lord,
  the Holy Spirit, the Paraclete;
Give me the spirit
  of wisdom and understanding,
  the spirit of counsel and fortitude,
  the spirit of knowledge and piety;
Fill me with
  the spirit of the fear of the Lord.

SPONSOR

Lord, look with love on your servant
and *their* family and friends.
May almighty God bless us all,
+ the Abba, and the Son,
  and the Holy Spirit.   R. **Amen.**

BLESSING of a NEW DRIVER
drawn from the blessing of pilgrims

PARENT

N., Christ, the Son of God, came into the world to gather those who were scattered and to call us to follow in his way. Taking on responsible freedom, you give honor to God, in whose image you are made. Thanks be to God.

INTERCESSIONS

Lord Jesus, you came as one like us and willed to live as we live; Grant that with you always at our side, we may walk gladly on our pilgrimage of faith; We pray to the Lord… R. Lord, hear our prayer.

Master Teacher, you went from town to town preaching your Gospel and healing the sick; May you still travel our roadways, and give us your strength; We pray to the Lord… R. Lord, hear our prayer.

Risen Lord, you were a companion to your disciples on the road to Emmaus; Bless all our journeys with hope; We pray to the Lord… R. Lord, hear our prayer.

Crucified Christ, you gave us to
your Mother, to be her children; Join in
her prayers and keep our driver safe;
We pray to the Lord… R. Lord, hear our prayer.

Lord Jesus, for the joys and concerns
of our hearts… *(PAUSE)*:
We pray to the Lord… R. Lord, hear our prayer.

PARENT

N., hold your license and keys
as we pray for God's help and blessing.

O God of boundless mercy and majesty,
neither distance nor time separate you
from those over whom you keep watch.
Your servant places *their* trust in you:
In every place stay close to *them*.
Be *their* leader and companion
wherever *they* go.
Let no adversity harm *them* nor
any obstacle hinder *them* on *their* way.
Make all things work for *their* well-being
so that whatever *they* rightly desire
they may successfully achieve,
through Christ our Lord. R. Amen.

MARRIAGE

✢ In the name of the Abba and of the Son
and of the Holy Spirit.   R. Amen.

May the peace of Christ, the love of Abba,
and their communion in the Holy Spirit
be with us all.   R. And with our Spirit.

Gathered in God's love,
surrounded by beauty,
and trusting in God's providence,
we celebrate the vocation of Marriage.

N. and N., the People of God share your joy with God, our source of love and fidelity, as today you establish between yourselves a lifelong partnership.

Let us pray.

Be attentive to our prayers, O God,
and in your kindness pour out your grace
on these your servants (N.___ and N.___),
that, coming together they may be
confirmed in their love for one another
through Christ our Lord.   R. Amen.

READING

A reading from the letter of Paul
to the Romans   8:35,37-39

What can separate us from the love of Christ? Will anguish, or distress, or persecution, or famine, or nakedness, or peril, or the sword?

No, in all these things we conquer overwhelmingly through him who loved us.

For I am convinced that neither death, nor life, nor angels, nor principalities, nor present things, nor future things, nor powers, nor height, nor depth, nor any other creature will be able to separate us from the love of God in Christ Jesus our Lord.

The Word of the Lord.   R. Thanks be to God.

OFFICIANT   N. & N.

N. & N., have you come here freely?   Yes

**Is it your intention to be spouses
to each other?**   Yes

**Are you ready to love and honor each other
for as long as you both shall live?**   Yes

(*Are you ready to accept children from God,
and to bring them up with loving kindness?* Yes)

**Join your hands and declare your consent
before God and God's people.**

CONSENTS

I, _____, take you, _____,
to be my *husband/wife/spouse*.
I promise to be faithful to you,
in good times and in bad,
in sickness and in health,
to love you and to honor you
all the days of my life.

PRAYER

May the God of Abraham and Sarah,
the God of Isaac and Rebecca,
the God of Jacob and Rachel,
God who joined together
our first parents in paradise,
strengthen and bless your consents.

RINGS

May the Lord bless these rings
which you will give to each other.

> N_____, receive this ring
> as a sign of my love and fidelity,
> in the name of the Abba,
> and of the Son,
> and of the Holy Spirit.

KISS

PRAYERS of the FAITHFUL

Brothers and Sisters, as witnesses to these promises
of lifelong fidelity, let us together give voice to prayer.
I will begin each petition:

1

We pray - *All:* **May all people of good will, especially
all who have accompanied N. & N. on their journey,
grow ever deeper in the faith, hope and love of Jesus.**

2

We pray - *All:* **May all leaders seek justice, build peace,
and work to eliminate poverty and intolerance.**

3

We pray - *All:* **May comfort, encouragement, patience,
mercy, and forgiveness abide in all families.**

4

We pray - *All:* **May each human being who is sick,
lonely, shamed, discouraged, oppressed or
pushed to the margins, find dignity as God's beloved
and friendship in God's colorful family.**

5

We pray - *All:* **May all who have gone before us in faith,
especially _____, all our ancestors,
and our friends we have been blessed to know,
feast at the heavenly banquet.**

6

We pray - *All:* **May N. & N. choose to love anew
with the dawn of each day and be ever blessed
in the prayers of their family and friends.**

7

We pray - *All:* **May the deepest desires of our hearts
be fulfilled, those prayers we hold in the center
of our souls where God speaks God's name.**

BLESSING

And join me in extending our hands over N. & N. for the traditional blessing:

**Holy and Mighty God, maker of the whole world,
who created human beings in your own image
and willed that we be crowned with your blessing,
we pray for these your servants,
who are joined today as spouses to each other.**

**May your abundant blessings, Lord,
come upon these companions for life,
and may the power of your Holy Spirit
set their hearts aflame from on high,
so that, living together as a family
 (*and entrusted with children*)
they may be a blessing to the People of God.**

**In happiness may they praise you, Lord,
in sorrow may they seek you out;
may they have the joy of your presence
to assist them in their toil,
and know that you are near
to comfort them in their need;
let them pray to you in the holy assembly
and bear witness to you in the world,
and after a happy old age,
together with their surrounding circle of friends,
may they come to the Reign of Heaven,
through Christ our Lord.**

R. Amen.

Together let us sing as Jesus taught us to pray:

> Our Father, who art in heaven;
> hallowed be thy name.
> Thy kingdom come. Thy will be done
> on earth as it is in heaven.
> Give us this day our daily bread,
> and forgive us our trespasses
> as we forgive those who trespass against us.
> And lead us not into temptation,
> but deliver us from evil.
> Amen.

FINAL BLESSING

Please respond with *"Amen."*

**May God the all-powerful Abba grant you joy
and bless you as a new family.** R. Amen.

**May the Only Begotten Son of God
dwell with you in good times and in bad.** R. Amen.

**May the Holy Spirit of God always
pour forth love into your hearts.** R. Amen.

**And may almighty God bless us all,
the + Abba, and the Son, and their Holy Spirit.**
 R. Amen.

I present to you _____

BLESSING of MARRIED COUPLES

I ask each of you who is married
and here today with your spouse
to stand and join your hands
and face each other.

Call to mind the day of your engagement.
(*pause*)   Please repeat after me:

> *Lord God . . .*
> *Creator and Abba of us all . . .*
> *thank you for the gift . . .*
> *of your providence . . .*
> *in letting us find each other . . .*

Call to mind now,
the day of your wedding celebration.
(*pause*)   Please repeat after me:

> *Lord Jesus Christ . . .*
> *Savior and Redeemer of us all . . .*
> *thank you for the gift . . .*
> *of your grace . . .*
> *in letting us forgive . . .*
> *and be forgiven . . .*

and stay committed in marriage . . .
and be your presence for each other . . .
Lord Jesus, you have promised us
  your grace . . .
and you have remained faithful to us . . .

**Be aware, now,
of where you are in this moment.**
(*pause*)   **Please repeat after me:**

Holy Spirit of God . . .
thank you for all of your help . . .
Be with us always . . .
for we know that we are weak . . .
and need your help every day . . .
Help us especially to live . . .
each day and in eternity . . .
in the love of the Abba and Son . . .
where you dwell in us now . . .

**Please continue holding hands
and facing each other
as we pray for you
and for all of God's children.**

**Abba all holy, you have made marriage
the great symbol of Christ's love for the
people of God; bestow on these your disciples
the fullness of your own love;
We pray to the Lord...** R. Lord, hear our prayer.

**You live in eternity
with the Son and the Holy Spirit
in oneness of life and communion of love;
grant that these your servants will be mindful
of the covenant of love they pledged to each
other and persevere in their fidelity;
We pray to the Lord...** R. Lord, hear our prayer.

**In your providence you have ordained
that all genuinely human experiences
should become ways of leading the faithful
to share in the mystery of Christ;
grant to these your apostles in the world
serenity in good times and in bad
and the will to stay close to Christ;
We pray to the Lord...** R. Lord, hear our prayer.

**It is your will that married life
should be a lesson in Christian living;
grant that all spouses may be witnesses
to the wonders of your Son's love;
We pray to the Lord...** R. Lord, hear our prayer.

Join me in extending hands in blessing:

We praise you, O God, we bless you, Creator of all things, who in the beginning made humans in your image that we might form a communion of life and love.

We also give you thanks for graciously blessing the family life of these your servants, so that it might present an image of Christ's union with the People of God.

Look with kindness upon them today, and as you have sustained their communion amid joys and struggles, renew their covenant each day, increase their charity, and strengthen in them the bond of peace so that together with the circle of (*children and*) family and friends that surrounds them they may for ever enjoy your blessing, through Christ our Lord. R. Amen.

We gather our prayers in the words Jesus gave us:

> *Our Father...*

May almighty God bless us all,
+ the Abba, and the Son,
   and the Holy Spirit. R. Amen.

PRAYERS for the SICK

Christ is always present
when we are gathered in his name;
today we welcome him especially
as physician and healer.

It is always appropriate to pray
for healing when in danger of death,
or before major surgery, or
when recovering from a serious illness.
It can also be right and good for us
to pray for the healing of those
who struggle with chronic illness, such as
depression, addiction, or chronic pain.
We pray that the sick may be restored to
health by the presence of the Risen Lord
and made whole in his fullness.

For all not in need of healing,
please offer a prayer of gratitude
for the gift of good health and,
open to the possibility
that you have been graced with
the charism of intercessory prayer, pray
for healing of your brothers and sisters.

Please respond, *"Lord have mercy."*

**God of love,
bless these good people and fill them
with new hope and strength:
   Lord, have mercy...**   R. Lord, have mercy.

**Relieve their pain:
   Lord, have mercy...**   R. Lord, have mercy.

**Assist all who care for the sick:
   Lord, have mercy...**   R. Lord, have mercy.

**Give life and health to our siblings
on whom we lay hands in your name:
   Lord, have mercy...**   R. Lord, have mercy.

LAYING ON of HANDS in SILENCE

**God of mercy, ease the sufferings
and comfort the weakness of your
servants for whom your people pray,
through Christ our Lord.**   R. Amen.

**May almighty God bless us all,
+ the Abba, and the Son,
   and the Holy Spirit.**   R. Amen.

BLESSING of TEACHERS
BEGINNING OF YEAR

Lord God, source of all wisdom and
knowledge, you sent your Son, Jesus Christ,
to live among us and to proclaim his
message of faith, hope, and love to all.
In your goodness bless our brothers and
sisters who offer themselves as teachers.
Strengthen them with your gifts
that they may teach by word and example
the truth which comes from you,
through Christ our Lord.   R. Amen.

BLESSING of TEACHERS & STUDENTS
END OF YEAR

We thank you and bless you, Lord our God.
In times past you spoke in many and varied
ways through the prophets, but in this final
age, you have spoken through your Son to
reveal to all peoples the riches of your grace.
May teachers and students who have met
to ponder creation and goodness
be filled with the knowledge of your will
in all wisdom and spiritual understanding,
and, pleasing you as we seek in all things,
bear fruit in every good work,
through Christ our Lord.   R. Amen.

BLESSING of an ADVENT WREATH

Lord our God,
we praise you for your Son, Jesus Christ:
he is Emmanuel, the hope of the peoples,
he is the wisdom that teaches and guides us,
he is the Savior of every nation.

Lord God, let your blessing come upon us
as we light the candles of this wreath.
May the wreath and its light be a sign
of Christ's promise to bring us salvation.
May he come quickly and not delay,
through Christ our Lord. R. Amen.

BLESSING of a NATIVITY SCENE

God of every nation and people, from the
very beginning of creation you have shown
us your love: when our need for a Savior
was great, you sent your Son to be born
of the Virgin Mary. To our lives he brings
joy and peace, justice and mercy, and love.

Lord, bless all who look upon this manger;
may it remind us of the humble birth of
Jesus, and raise up our thoughts to him, who
is God-with-us and Savior of all, and who
lives and reigns for ever and ever. R. Amen.

BLESSING of a BIBLE

Blessed be your name, O Lord.
You are the fount and source of every
blessing, and you look with delight
upon the devout practices of the faithful.
Draw near, we pray, to your servant
and, as *they* use this Bible
in building up *their* faith and devotion,
grant that *they* may also strive to be
transformed into the likeness of Christ,
your Son, who lives and reigns with you
for ever and ever. R. Amen.

BLESSING of a VEHICLE

All-powerful God, Creator
of heaven and earth, in the rich depths
of your wisdom you have empowered us
to produce great and beautiful works.
Grant, we pray, that those
who use this vehicle may travel safely
and with care for the safety of others.
Whether they travel for business or
pleasure, let them always find Christ
to be the companion of their journey,
who lives and reigns with you
for ever and ever. R. Amen.

BLESSING of a MOTHER
SECOND SUNDAY OF MAY

Loving God, as a mother gives
life and nourishment to her children,
so you watch over your Church.

Bless this woman, that she may be
strengthened as a Christian mother.

Let the example of her faith and love
shine forth.

Grant that we, (*her sons and daughters*),
may honor her always
with a spirit of profound respect,
through Christ our Lord.   R. Amen.

BLESSING of a FATHER
THIRD SUNDAY OF JUNE

God our Father, in your wisdom and love
you made all things.

Bless this man, that he may be
strengthened as a Christian father.

Let the example of his faith and love
shine forth.

Grant that we, (*his sons and daughters*),
may honor him always
with a spirit of profound respect,
through Christ our Lord.   R. Amen.

COMMENDATION of the DYING

**Grace to us and peace
from God our Father
and the Lord Jesus Christ.**

℟. **And with our spirit.**

To you, O Lord, I lift up my soul.
Psalm 25:1

The Lord Jesus says,
today you will be with me in paradise.
Luke 23:43

Into your hands, Lord,
I commend my spirit.
Psalm 31:5a

The Lord is my shepherd…
Psalm 23

In was now around midday…
Luke 23:44-49

Do not let your hearts be troubled…
John 14:1-6,23,27

CANTICLE of SIMEON
Lord, now you let your servant go in peace;
my eyes have seen the salvation
which you have prepared
before the face of all the peoples,
a light for revelation to the nations
and glory for your people, Israel.
Luke 2:29-32

OUR FATHER

HAIL MARY

PRAYER of COMMENDATION

**Lord Jesus Christ, our Redeemer,
we pray for your servant N.,
and commend *him/her* to your mercy.
For *his/her* sake you came from heaven;
when you are ready, Lord,
receive *him/her* into the joy of your reign.
For though *he/she* has sinned,
he/she has not denied
the Father, the Son, and the Holy Spirit,
but has believed in God
and has worshipped *his/her* Creator.**

DOXOLOGY

**Glory be to the Father, and to the Son,
and to the Holy Spirit,
as it was in the beginning,
is now, and every shall be,
world without end.**   R. Amen.

**May almighty God bless *N.* and us all,
+ the Father, and the Son,
   and the Holy Spirit.**   R. Amen.

VIGIL for the DECEASED

Grace to us and peace from God our Abba
and our Lord Jesus Christ.

                          R. And with our spirit.

The ties of friendship and affection
do not unravel with death.
Confident that God remembers the good
we do and forgives our sins,
let us pray,
asking God to gather N._____ to Godself.

    May we pray for a moment in silence...

Lord our God,
the death of our *brother/sister* N.___
recalls our human condition
and the brevity of our lives on earth.
But for those who believe in your love
death is not the end,
nor does it destroy the bonds
that you forge in our lifetimes.
Bring the light of Christ's resurrection
to this moment as we pray for N.
and for those who love *him/her*,
through Christ our Lord.   R. Amen.

A reading from the second letter
of Saint Paul to the Corinthians   5:1,6-9

> We know that
> if our earthly tent-house should be destroyed
> we have a building from God,
> a house not made with hands,
> eternal in the heaven.
>   So we are always confident,
> knowing that at home in the body
> we are away from the Lord,
> for we walk by faith, not by sight.
>   Yet we are confident,
> and would rather leave the home of our body
> and be at home with the Lord.
>   And so, whether at home or away from home,
> we aspire to be well pleasing to God.

The Word of the Lord.   R. **Thanks be to God.**

ROSARY and/or REMARKS of REMEMBRANCE

LITANY of INTERCESSION

Trusting in God's mercy,
we call on Christ Jesus
for the greatest of all gifts
that is the mercy of God:

> Risen Lord, pattern of our life for ever:
> Lord, have mercy...   R. Lord, have mercy.
>
> Promise and image of what we shall be:
> Lord, have mercy...   R. Lord, have mercy.
>
> Word of God who delivered us
> from the fear of death:
> Lord, have mercy...   R. Lord, have mercy.
>
> Lord Jesus, you bless those
> who mourn and are in pain.
> Bless N.'s family and friends
> who gather today.
> Lord, have mercy...   R. Lord, have mercy.

We pray for the coming of
the reign of God as Jesus taught us:

Our Father . . .

CONCLUDING PRAYER

**Lord Jesus, our Redeemer,
you willingly gave yourself up to death
that all might be saved
and pass from death to life.
We humbly ask you to comfort your
servants in their grief and to receive N.
into the arms of your mercy.
You alone are the Holy One,
you are mercy itself;
Forgive N.** *his/her* **sins, and grant** *him/her*
**a place of happiness, light, and peace
in the reign of your glory
for ever and ever.** R. Amen.

Eternal rest grant unto *him/her*, **O Lord.**
R. **And let perpetual light shine upon** *him/her*.

May *he/she* **rest in peace.** R. Amen.

May *his/her* **soul
and the souls of all the faithful departed,
through the mercy of God,
rest in peace.** R. Amen.

We go in peace. R. Thanks be to God.

FUNERAL at a GRAVESIDE

The grace of our Lord Jesus Christ,
and the love of God,
and the communion of the Holy Spirit
be with us all. R. And with our spirit.

SPRINKLING COFFIN

In the waters of baptism
N. died with Christ
and rose with him to new life.
May *he/she* now share with him
eternal glory.

OR CREMATED REMAINS

As our *brother/sister* N.
has died with the Lord, so may
he/she live with him in glory.

PLACING of the PALL and/or CHRISTIAN SYMBOLS

INVITATION TO PRAYER

We believe that in death life is changed,
not ended, and so we come together
to renew our trust in Christ
who, by dying on the cross, has freed us
from eternal death and, by rising,
has opened for us the gates of heaven.

Let us take a moment of silence to pray
for our *brother/sister*, and for ourselves.

PAUSE

OUTSIDE EASTER TIME

O God, almighty Abba, our faith professes
that your Son died and rose again;
mercifully grant that through this mystery
your servant N.___,
who has fallen asleep in Christ,
may rejoice to rise again through him,
who lives and reigns with you in the unity
of the Holy Spirit, God, for ever and ever.

R. Amen.

DURING EASTER TIME

Listen kindly to our prayers, O Lord:
as our faith in your Son,
raised from the dead, is deepened,
may our hope of resurrection
for your departed servant N.___
also find new strength,
through our Lord Jesus Christ, your Son,
who lives and reigns with you in the unity
of the Holy Spirit, God, for ever and ever.

R. Amen.

Let us listen to the word of God.

SAMPLE READINGS

A reading from the Book
of the prophet Isaiah 25:6a,7-9

> On this mountain the L<small>ORD</small> of hosts
> will prepare a feast for all peoples.
>
> And on this mountain
> destroy the veil that veils all peoples,
> the web that is woven over all nations,
> and destroy death to forever.
>
> The L<small>ORD</small> God will wipe away
> the tears from every face
> and remove the shame of all people
> all over the earth;
> the L<small>ORD</small> has spoken.
>
> On that day it will be said:
> "Behold our God, to whom we looked to save us!
> This is the L<small>ORD</small> to whom we looked;
> let us rejoice and be glad
> in the salvation of our God!"

The word of the Lord.   R. **Thanks be to God.**

A RESPONSORIAL

PSALM 23

The Lord is my shepherd;
nothing shall I lack.

> R. **The Lord is my shepherd; nothing shall I lack.**

My Lord lays me down in green pastures
and leads me beside still quiet waters,
restoring my soul
and guiding me in paths of justice
for the Lord's own namesake.

> R. **The Lord is my shepherd; nothing shall I lack.**

So when I walk in the deep dark valley
I will not fear for you are with me,
your rod and staff a comfort to me.

> R. **The Lord is my shepherd; nothing shall I lack.**

A table you prepare before me
in the presence even of enmity.
My head you anoint with oil
and my cup is overflowing.

> R. **The Lord is my shepherd; nothing shall I lack.**

Surely goodness and love will follow me
all the days of my life
and I will dwell in the Lord's own house
for the length of my days.

> R. **The Lord is my shepherd; nothing shall I lack.**

GOSPEL

A reading from the holy Gospel
    according to John   14:1-6a

Jesus said to his disciples:
"Do not let your heart be troubled;
believe in God, believe also in me.
In my Abba's house there are many abiding places.
If not, would I have told you
that I am going to prepare a place for you?
And if I go and prepare a place for you,
I will come back again and receive you to myself,
that where I am you also may be.
Where I am going you know the way."
    Thomas said to him,
"Lord, we do not know where you are going;
how do we know the way?"
    Jesus said to him,
"I am the way and the truth and the life."

OR

A reading from the holy Gospel
    according to Luke   24:13-16,28-35

On the same first day of the week,
two of Jesus' disciples journeyed
to a village named Emmaus,
seven miles from Jerusalem,
and they were talking to each other
about the things that had occurred.

And it happened
that while they were talking and discussing,
Jesus himself drawing near journeyed with them,
but their eyes were held from recognizing him.

Drawing near to the village to which they were
journeying, he pretended to journey farther.
But they urged him, "Remain with us,
for it is toward evening and the day has declined."
So he went in to remain with them.

And it happened that while he
reclined with them, taking the bread, he blessed,
and having broken he handed it to them.

Their eyes were opened and they recognized
him, but he became invisible to them.

They said to each other, "Was not our heart
burning in us as he spoke to us on the way
and opened up to us the Scriptures?"

Rising up in the same hour,
they returned to Jerusalem and found
the eleven gathered and those with them saying,
"Truly the Lord has been raised
and has appeared to Simon!"

Then the two related
what happened on the way,
how he was known to them
in the breaking of the bread.

The gospel of the Lord.
>R. **Praise to you, Lord Jesus Christ.**

HOMILY OR WORDS of REMEMBRANCE

PRAYER of the FAITHFUL

**God, the almighty Abba,
raised Christ his Son from the dead;
with confidence we ask God
to save all people, living and dead:**

FAMILY MEMBER?

**For N. who in baptism was given
the promise of eternal life;
may *he/she* now be admitted
to the communion of saints;
We pray to the Lord.** R. Lord, hear our prayer.

**For our *brother/sister*
who ate the bread of life;
may *he/she* be raised up on the last day;
We pray to the Lord.** R. Lord, hear our prayer.

**For our deceased family and friends
and for all who have helped us;
may they have
the reward of their goodness;
We pray to the Lord.** R. Lord, hear our prayer.

For the family and friends
of our *brother/sister* N.___ ;
may they be consoled in their grief
by the Lord, who wept
at the death of his friend Lazarus;
We pray to the Lord.   R. Lord, hear our prayer.

For all of us assembled here in faith;
may we be gathered together again
in the reign of God;
We pray to the Lord.   R. Lord, hear our prayer.

CONCLUSION

God, our shelter and our strength,
hear the prayers we offer
for our departed brothers and sisters.
Cleanse them from their sins and
grant them the fullness of redemption,
through Christ our Lord.   R. Amen.

With longing
for the coming of the reign of God,
let us pray as Jesus taught us:
                              Our Father…

AT the REMAINS

**Before we go our separate ways,
let us take leave of our *brother/sister*.
May our farewell
express our affection for *him/her*,
ease our sadness,
and strengthen our hope
that we shall joyfully greet *him/her* again
when the love of Christ,
which conquers all things,
destroys even death itself.**

(Please stand, and)
let us pray for a moment in silence.

INCENSE and SONG of FAREWELL

**May the angels lead you into paradise
and the Saints meet you at your arrival.**

> R. *Receive his/her soul and present him/her to God the Most High.*

**May the angels lead you to the holy city
and Christ Jesus take you to himself.**

> R. *Receive...*

**Eternal rest grant unto *him/her*, O Lord,
and let perpetual light shine upon *him/her*.**

> R. *Receive...*

PRAYER of COMMENDATION

Into your hands, Abba of mercies,
we commend our *brother/sister* N.___
in the sure and certain hope that,
together with all who have died in Christ,
he/she will rise with him on the last day.

[We give you thanks for the blessings you
bestowed upon N. in this life: they are
signs to us of your goodness and of our
communion with the saints in Christ.]

Merciful Lord, turn toward us and listen
to our prayers: open the gates of paradise
to your servant and help us who remain
to comfort one another with assurances of
faith, until we all meet in Christ and are
with you and with our *brother/sister* for
ever, through Christ our Lord.   R. Amen.

CLOSING PRAYERS, go to page 85

OR IF BURIAL IS AT ANOTHER PLACE

In peace let us take our *brother/sister*
to *his/her* place of rest.

OR IF COMMITTAL IS DELAYED

In the sure hope of the resurrection, we take
leave of our *brother/sister*: let us go in peace.

COMMITTAL IF LATER at the GRAVE

**Our *brother/sister* N._ has gone
  to *his/her* rest in the peace of Christ.
May the Lord now welcome *him/her*
  to the table of God's children in heaven.
With faith and hope in eternal life,
  let us assist *him/her* with our prayers.**

**Let us pray to the Lord also for ourselves.
May we who mourn be
  reunited one day with our *brother/sister*;
  together may we meet Christ Jesus
  when he who is our life appears in glory.**

COMMITTAL AT THE GRAVE & COMMENDATION OF CREMATED REMAINS

**In sure and certain hope of the resurrection
  to eternal life through our Lord Jesus
  Christ, we commend to Almighty God
  our *brother/sister* N._ ,
  and we commit *his/her* earthly remains
  to the ground [*or the deep, or their resting place*]:
  earth to earth, ashes to ashes, dust to dust.
The Lord bless *him/her* and keep *him/her*,
  the Lord make his face to shine upon
  him/her and be gracious to *him/her*,
  the Lord lift up his countenance
  upon *him/her* and give *him/her* peace.**

LITANY of INTERCESSION

**For our *brother/sister* N.___ ,
once more we call on the mercy of God,
as we pray to our Lord Jesus Christ,
who said,** Matthew 25:34
 *Come, you who are blessed by my Abba;
 inherit the realm prepared for you
 from the foundation of the world.*

Please repeat after me:
 "Lord, have mercy."
 R. Lord, have mercy.

**Lord, you raised the dead to life;
give to our *brother/sister* eternal life;**
 Lord, have mercy...   R. Lord, have mercy.

**Our *brother/sister* was washed in baptism
and anointed with the Holy Spirit; give
him/her communion with all your saints;**
 Lord, have mercy...   R. Lord, have mercy.

***He/she* was nourished with your body
and blood; grant *him/her* a place at the
table in your heavenly reign.**
 Lord, have mercy...   R. Lord, have mercy.

**Comfort us in our sorrow;
let our faith be our consolation,
and eternal life our hope..
   Lord, have mercy...**   R. Lord, have mercy.

**With longing
for the coming of the reign of God,
we pray:**
   All: ***Our Father . . .***

REMAINS ARE SPRINKLED WITH HOLY WATER

CONCLUDING PRAYER

**God of holiness and power,
   accept our prayers on behalf of
   your servant N. ;
in *his/her* heart
   he/she desired to do your will.
As *his/her* faith united *him/her*
   to your people on earth,
so may your mercy join *him/her*
   to the angels in heaven,
through Christ our Lord.**   R. Amen.

CLOSING PRAYERS

Eternal rest grant unto *him/her*, O Lord.

> R. **And let perpetual light shine upon *him/her*.**

May *he/she* rest in peace.   R. **Amen.**

**May *his/her* soul
and the souls of all the faithful departed,
through the mercy of God, rest in peace.**

> R. **Amen.**

LAY FAITHFUL SIGNING HIMSELF/HERSELF

**May the peace of God,
which is beyond all understanding,
keep our hearts and minds
in the knowledge and love of God
and of his Son, our Lord Jesus Christ.**

**And may God bless us all
+ in the name of the Father,
and of the Son,
and of the Holy Spirit.**   R. **Amen.**

We go in peace...   R. **Thanks be to God.**

FOR VOCATIONS

ORDINARY TIME

Abba, you call us to the table of your Son,
renew us by word and sacrament,
and send us to labor in your harvest.

We are a people in need of the witness
of faithful marriages and priests,
generous single people and deacons,
religious sisters, brothers, monks and nuns.

Help each disciple to trust in your call,
make us able and willing to do what you ask,
keep us united in our gifted diversity,
and bring to maturity every seed you sow…

ADVENT & CHRISTMAS

Abba, you call us
to prepare the way for Christ our Lord,
bringing low the mountains of our pride
and filling up the valleys of our weakness.

As you created us in your own image,
open our minds and hearts
to know our longing for the Savior.

Help us to follow the example of Mary,
always ready to do your will.

As we celebrate the simple beauty of the
Incarnation of your Son, help us in freedom
to say "yes" to our vocations
and make us radiant with his light…

LENT

O God of compassion, through honest
awareness of sin and the grace of repentance
you protect us from what could harm us
and lead us to what will save us.

Your Son, Jesus Christ, accepted the cross
and redeemed your sons and daughters.

Through prayer, fasting, and almsgiving
you call us each to a unique vocation
of health, healing and mercy.

May we embrace the paschal mystery
and, faithful to the gospel of Christ,
become a people who worship you
in spirit and in truth…

EASTER

Loving Abba, send your Holy Spirit
to fill the hearts of your faithful
and set fire in us your confirming love.

Give us wisdom to seek your face,
understanding of our baptism in Christ, and
right judgment to discern his call in freedom.

Give us courage to say yes to our vocations,
knowledge of what Jesus teaches,
and reverence for the ways of the Abba.

Give us wonder and awe in your presence,
that the witness we give to the resurrection of
the Son may be pleasing to you, Abba, and help
the Holy Spirit renew the face of the earth…

BLESSING of WATER
DURING EASTER TIME

Lord our God,
you created water for life and healing,
to make the fields fruitful,
and to refresh and cleanse our bodies.

You used waters of mercy
to free your people from slavery
and quench their thirst in the desert.

Christ made holy the waters of the Jordan,
renewing our nature in cleansing regeneration.

Remembering again
your wondrous work of creation
and your even greater work of redemption,
we ask you to bless this water.

May it remind us always
of the Baptism we have received
and our anointing into our Savior's vocation
of priest, prophet and royal:
as ministers ever washing the feet of humanity,
disciples still learning at the feet of the Son,
and apostles sent all over the cosmos
to give witness to his resurrection,
who lives and reigns with you
in the unity of the Holy Spirit,
God for ever and ever. R. Amen.

UNIVERSAL PRAYERS of the FAITHFUL

Let us pray to God who graciously listened
to the prayers and deepest desires
of the beloved Son:

> For the shepherds of souls,
> that they may serve with wisdom
> the people entrusted to them; *We pray…*
>
> For the whole world,
> that all may come to know
> the peace given by Christ; *We pray…*
>
> For our brothers and sisters who suffer,
> that their sorrow may be turned to the joy
> that no one can take from them; *We pray…*
>
> For our own community, that it may
> bear witness with great confidence
> to the enduring love of God; *We pray…*
>
> For all who have gone before us, that they
> may see God face to face; *We pray…*

O God, hear the desires of all who seek you
and the prayers of all who cry to you
as we seek your will in all we say and do
through Christ our Lord.   R. Amen.

www.ingramcontent.com/pod-product-compliance
Lightning Source LLC
Chambersburg PA
CBHW030531080526
44586CB00011B/398